THE TALE OF THREE DOGS

by

ALICK HARTLEY

Illustrated by

WENDY HOWARD

Edited by

RACHEL HEWITT

Chapter 1 SALLY

It all began within a few days of the third anniversary of the death of my wife. At that time, I was working each afternoon as a Branch Treasurer of the British Red Cross. Apart from that, I was trying to write some Mathematics books, intended specifically for overseas - the developing world. The "Teasmade" had made tea at 6.30 a.m., a legacy from the days when my wife and I were teachers. I was just lying in bed, although I had things to do, there was no one for whom to get up.

I was suddenly startled by the doorbell. After making myself presentable, I opened the door to find a young man on the threshold. He asked me if I was the owner of a little puppy, which had been following him as he walked along the main road, the A483 from Shrewsbury to Aberystwyth. As it is a very busy road, he was concerned for its safety.

I replied that it was not mine, but that it might belong to my next-door neighbours. I knew that they had two cats - I had once been asked to feed and water them when they were away for a few days - but I did not think that they had a dog. However, as there was a young family, I thought that the puppy could have been a recent acquisition.

I told the young man - a student on his way to the college - that if the puppy did not belong to my neighbours and he brought it back to me, I would look after it and telephone the police. Clearly the student wanted to get on his way to the College just up the road. Some minutes later, back he came and I was left in charge of the puppy.

I often wonder if that student knows what chain of events were triggered off by his kind and unselfish action. Perhaps that is a lesson in itself - just how one simple little action may play an important part in God's plan for somebody.

I immediately phoned the Police Station and tried to describe the puppy. I did not recognise the breed at all, but told the Police that it was like a Fox Terrier but with a longer body and short legs more like a Dachshund. They asked me to keep it for the time being. I told them that I had to go into the Red Cross office after lunch, but that I could keep it until then and bring it in to them on my way to work.

So I coped with the puppy until lunchtime. It was not very well-behaved, no young puppies are, but I became quite fond of it. When I handed it in to the Police, the Police Officer said straight away "It's a Jack Russell bitch." He took my name, address and phone number and said that they would keep it in their kennels for one week. Then, unless it had been claimed, they would have to dispose of it. I could easily guess just what that implied.

I tried to put the puppy to the back of my mind until the following Thursday. Then I phoned the Police to ask if it had been claimed - the answer was "No". It then seemed likely that it was not going to be claimed. So I then began to wonder what I should do - whether I should offer it a home. Half of me was hoping that it would be claimed so that there would be no question of my having it - I would not have the responsibility for it. Half of me was wishing that it would not be claimed so that it could stay with me.

From the human point of view, there was **every** reason why I should not have a dog.

Firstly, I have Chronic Lymphatic Leukaemia which means that I have less than the normal resistance to infection. The Church that I attend used to use common Communion goblets instead of individual cups. At that time, I was so conscious of my problem that I took the bread but declined to take the wine. It goes without saying that the presence of a dog in the house gives much more chance of infection.

Secondly, at that time, I was taking Beta-blockers as I had been diagnosed as having Angina.

Thirdly, visits to my sister-in-law and her family demonstrated clearly that I have some allergy where dogs are concerned. They had a Welsh Springer which I liked very much. I seemed to be all right for a day or two with them. Any longer than that, my eyes used to be affected and I used to sneeze a lot. I understand that it is not the dog itself or even the dog's hairs that cause the problem but some very tiny creatures which live amongst the dog's hairs. When I was young, I was asthmatic. I can still remember one night struggling to breathe, literally fighting for my life. I often wonder now whether that was caused by our dog. There is a close link between asthma and allergies.

Lastly, at that time I had no back garden. The garden around my bungalow was completely "open plan". It was then possible to walk right round the bungalow. More importantly, by whichever door a puppy got out of the bungalow, it could run straight out onto the busy main road. So it was **not** the best or safest place to bring up a puppy.

I cannot truthfully say that I remember consciously praying about the puppy. Isn't it true that we tend to pray for what we think we need or what we believe that others need? Shouldn't we pray most when we don't even know what we need? I have been greatly blessed by the Lord but I find that what I need most of all is guidance from the Lord as to what He wants me to do. Perhaps in the matter of the puppy, I had been content just to leave it entirely to the Lord.

God clearly had **very** different ideas about the situation. When I called in at the Police Station on the Saturday morning, I was told that the puppy had still not been claimed. I could only believe that it was the Lord's will that I should have it. I arranged a suitable time to collect the puppy on the following Monday evening. Then I did the necessary shopping - collar, name disc, lead, food, eating bowl, drinking bowl and a dog basket.

I was given directions how to get to the kennels and so, after work on Monday, I set off to find the place. The kennels were way up in the hills above Montgomery, so high up that they were above the snow line. We had seen no snow at all down in Newtown. I signed a receipt and collected the puppy. I took her home and was led to call her "Sally". I was truly blessed that my bungalow had a small laundry/utility room with a tiled floor, ideal for a dog's bedroom.

From that moment on, my life began to change beyond recognition.

Instead of lying in bed until I really felt that I just had to get up, I roused myself early to take the puppy out. I began to realise how ideal a place I lived in, from the point of view of rearing and exercising a dog. I had the choice of several lovely riverside walks, a different walk for different times of the day.

The pre-breakfast walk was westward along the main road, the A483, over a footbridge across the railway, through a housing estate, eastward - downstream - along a riverside path and then back home westward along the main road. It was on this walk that I first saw swans on the River Severn. Almost all God's creatures have some kind of beauty, but swans gliding on the river have a particular beauty and elegance.

I said "almost all" because I have to confess that I am repelled rather than attracted by snakes. To me, they look **evil**.

"....You will crawl on your belly and you will eat dust all the days of your life."

Genesis 3:14

After breakfast, I walked eastward along the main road and then - downstream - along the South side of the river to a footbridge across the river in town, returning home by the same route.

Walking on the edge of football fields, I saw a greater variety of slugs than I had ever seen before. I had thought that there were just snails - with houses - and slugs - without houses. Now I saw slugs in so many different sizes and so many different colours.

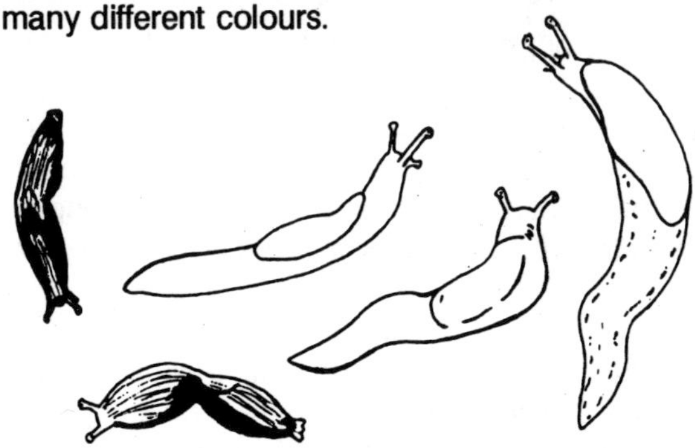

In some places, I saw how rapidly and efficiently slugs seemed to attack and clean up dog dirt. Most of us think of slugs as just a menace in our gardens, but they seem to perform very useful work as well : work that doesn't get done if slugs are all killed off by "chemicals".

After lunch and again in late afternoon, I drove into town, parked the car in the main car park and crossed the river by a footbridge and into the beautiful Dolerw Park on the North side of the river. The park is ideal for dogs as it is sheltered from both urban traffic and rural sheep. Squirrels may be glimpsed on or near the beautiful trees.

At the western end of the park is a wooded slope occupied by rabbits. At breeding time, many young rabbits can be seen eating and playing on the grass.

At the weekend, for a change, I drove to the other car park in town - I call it the Post Office car park. I crossed the river by a footbridge and then walked eastward - further downstream - along a riverside path on the North side of the river. Sometimes, the swans could be seen on that stretch of river.

For some time, I had been truly thankful that the Lord had led my wife and myself to Newtown in Mid-Wales before my wife was called home. Now I was more thankful than ever.

Walking by the river after breakfast, I passed many riverside trees. There I heard a greater variety of bird songs than I had ever heard before. How much of God's creation we miss if we spend all our time indoors.

During those first few weeks with Sally, almost everyone we met said that she was GORGEOUS. I could have sold her dozens of times. I bored my friends by saying that she was special. How gracious God is - He could have accomplished His purposes by sending me any old mongrel. I am sure that I would still have loved it, kept it and allowed it to change my life. But God is always more generous than is needed or than we deserve.

After a few weeks, the Lord made it clear to me what a poor witness I was, how many opportunities I had thrown away. So many times I had had to recount the story of how I acquired Sally, how I came to have a dog. To my shame, I had merely said "Sally followed a student along Llanidloes Road and he brought her to me" instead of saying "Sally is a gift from God to dispel my desperate loneliness, particularly at the weekend. A student brought her to my door."

For many of us, it is far from easy to talk about the Lord and our faith in Him. Do we seize all the opportunities to witness that are dangled in front of us?

Sally was not always well behaved. One fault was eating dog dirt. Apparently many puppies do it, but that is no consolation. I still loved Sally, but I couldn't bear her near me when she was contaminated with and smelling of dirt. I thought that that must be just how God feels when we are contaminated and "smelling" of sin. He will still love us but not want us close to Him.

One dog-walker told me it was the lack of some vitamin from their diet, which could be rectified by giving them yeast tablets. Yeast certainly helps but there are still occasions when the temptation is too great for her to resist. How familiar that sounds!

Another of her faults was not coming back to me to be put on her lead when it was time to go home. When we had walked straight from home, the walk sometimes ended with Sally sneaking along, dangerously off the lead, some distance behind me.

Sometimes, even worse happened after a walk in Dolerw Park. She would not come back to get into the car to be driven back home. Words cannot express the feeling of frustration, irritation and helplessness when you are defied by a tiny little puppy. I felt "I could murder her!" but thankfully I didn't really mean it. If a dog is punished for not coming back, it is even less likely to come back next time, particularly if you speak sharply to it. I found that it was better to hide my feelings completely and call her gently "Come on, precious" or "Come on, lovely". I now always give her a treat when she is back in the boot of my car.

However, immediately after such incidents, I was reluctant to let the dog off the lead ever again. She was no longer considered trustworthy. Misbehaviour results in loss of freedom and fun. The better the behaviour of the dog, the more freedom it can be allowed. Isn't it just the same with us? If we truly seek to do the Lord's will, the more freedom He will allow us.

Once our trust in a dog has been so destroyed that we no longer let it off the lead, how can it prove that it is trustworthy? We just have to give it a second chance and a third chance and a fourth chance.

Then Peter came to Jesus and asked, "Lord, how many times shall I forgive my brother when he sins against me? Up to seven times?" Jesus answered, " I tell you not seven times, but seventy-seven times."

Matthew 18:21,22

What a good job it is that God is even more gracious with us!

Bad behaviour seemed to happen most on Sundays. It seemed that just as God can use dogs or other animals to achieve his purposes, so also Satan can make use of them to try to thwart God's will.

I can particularly remember two occasions when Sally had been lagging behind, probably she had been "up to something". Thinking that she might be in trouble, she was reluctant to come back to me. This got her into more trouble than she was already.

How often do we get ourselves into even more sin by trying to cover up instead of confessing what we have done?

"Then the man and his wife heard the sound of the Lord God as he was walking in the garden in the cool of the day, and they hid from the Lord God among the trees of the garden."

Genesis 3:8

On one occasion, when we had reached an impasse, we were only reconciled because she went near a man lying down under a tree reading a book. Yes, it was summer! He grabbed her and returned her to me. I had not been able to make her understand that, regardless of what she had been up to, I only wanted her back with me.

On another occasion, Sally escaped into the river. She was clever enough - or should I say cunning enough - to realise that, in the river, she was safe from my clutches. Again, it was summer and I was wearing sandals.

There she was, standing in the river, unable to sit down, shivering with cold or fear or both, yet refusing to "surrender". I too refused to give in and stayed on the river bank opposite her.

This time, the deadlock was only broken by a young girl who was paddling in the river close by.

On each occasion, once I had got my hands on her, I could hug her and lovingly carry her back to the car. Everything was forgiven now that we were together again.

Does God feel that He doesn't care what we have done as long as we are reconciled and walking with Him again?

The second occasion particularly reminded me of our Lord Jesus Christ, by whom we sinners were reconciled to God and without whom we should still be "in the river".

Only Jesus could provide the bridge, the link, between God and mankind. Jesus did not just give a few minutes of His time to help a little dog in trouble, He endured torment, punishment and an agonizing death to save a world in trouble. Sadly, most of the world is still in trouble.

....

At home, it was a delight to play with Sally. Her favourite pastime involved me throwing a ball to the top of the stairs so that she had to run up to get it. Of course, she did not bring it back down to me. I had to go up the stairs myself to retrieve it and then throw it down for her to chase again. You will have surmised that I was getting at least as much exercise as she was - which did me the world of good.

Sally also liked "hide and seek" and a tug-of-war. Imagine a 67 year old having a tug-of-war with a tiny Jack Russell!

When I was using a computer to write a Statistics textbook - specifically for the developing world - Sally used to jump onto and play on the keyboard.

She frequently sat at the top of the stairs, surveying the world beneath her. If ever she was in the bungalow but out of sight, that is where I would find her. I suppose that, being so small, down on the ground she gets a very limited view of things.

Sally used to go to the Red Cross with me. There was a cat basket, rather like a rectangular birdcage, under my desk. Most of the time she would just sleep quietly and unnoticed, but occasionally she would express her displeasure of a visitor to the office or protest that she wanted or needed to go out.

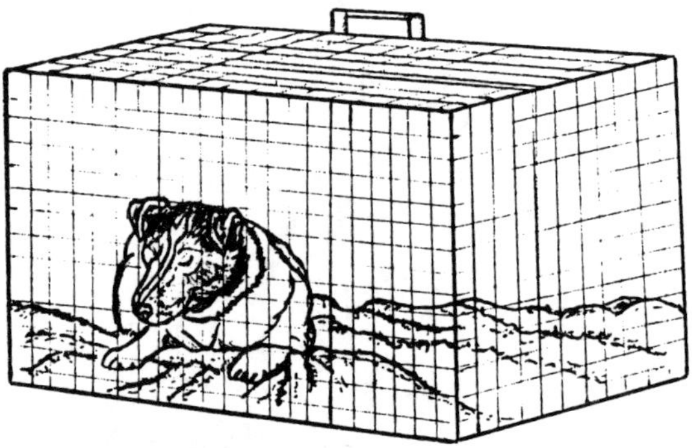

At this time, due to the exercise and fresh air that I was getting, whether it was fine, raining or snowing, my physical health was improving visibly. I was losing weight, to the eventual delight of the Haematology Department of Shrewsbury Hospital and my G.P. I could also get into clothes that I had not been able to wear for years. Physically, I was given a new life.

My "mental health" also improved. As I have already hinted, before Sally came I used to hate the weekends. I worked at the Red Cross during the week, but Friday evening was like the edge of a cliff. I could go out shopping in order to talk to somebody. I had the radio on constantly - I could not bear a silent house.

I was sometimes invited for Sunday lunch, but, after Kath died, I completely lost my confidence to go anywhere. I have heard of other widowers who have suffered in the same way. I also felt uncomfortable because I was unable to offer similar hospitality in return. Perhaps we have to learn to receive unhesitantly - where appropriate - as well as give unhesitantly.

Now my situation was completely different. The weekend offered the chance to spend more time with Sally. Instead of a yawning chasm, it became a welcome break and a change. I was never alone.

From my personal experience, I would say, to bereavement counsellors and pastors, encourage those who are left alone by bereavement to adopt a dog. If they are really not fit enough to cope with a dog - some might say that I was not - then suggest a cat or even a budgie.

I don't mean that they should spend a lot of money on a dog. Take them out for a run in the car and "just happen" to call on an RSPCA or NATIONAL CANINE DEFENCE LEAGUE animal home. They might be tempted to adopt and give a new life to a "rescue dog". I am certain that nothing could be better for them than to have a friend to give them companionship, a friend that they could love and for which they would have to care. Caring for and loving someone or some thing is the best cure for sadness and self-pity.

More important still, my spiritual health was improving. The Counsellor, the Holy Spirit, was giving me increased resistance against those personal private sins known only to God Himself and to me. I knew that I was daily getting closer to God. Spiritually also I was given a new life. It was some years since I had committed myself to the Lord and had accepted adult baptism. I now believe that first commitment is like passing a driving test, which does NOT mean that you are a good, experienced driver. It just means that you are good enough to be let loose on the roads on your own so that you can continue learning.

I had been a regular attender at Church, the Church Treasurer and a Deacon, but I now realise just how far from the Lord I had been. To get really close to the Lord requires not just that first commitment but **total** commitment.

I was starting to receive lots of ideas for Christian and Educational books, usually when I was out with Sally. When you receive ideas straight into the brain - I do not hear an audible voice - it is important to discern whether they come from God or from Satan. Usually, that is not difficult. You can test the ideas against the guiding principles given in the Scriptures.

You can also test them by the effect that the ideas, if carried out, would produce. If the effects would enhance the spreading of the Gospel and familiarity with the Scriptures, then the ideas must come from God. If they would adversely affect the spreading and learning of the Word, then the ideas must come from Satan.

"Test everything. Hold on to the good. Avoid every kind of evil."

1 Thessalonians 5:21,22

A difficult time for the owner of a female dog is when the dog is in season. Unless the owner wishes the dog to have puppies, she has to be kept away from male dogs. There are still quite a few dogs allowed to wander about on their own. I was greatly blessed with Sally. She seemed to resent the attentions of male dogs.

Sally thinks that, if she is kept on the lead, it is a punishment because she has done something wrong. So I am very reluctant to keep her on the lead - except near traffic - unless it is essential. If I thought that "the coast was clear", I would let her off the lead. Sometimes I would be caught off guard and a male dog would appear from nowhere. My anxieties proved quite ill-founded. I have seen dogs as big as a Labrador being chased right across a football pitch by little Sally!

Chapter 2 HEATHER

After some time, it was made clear to me that it might not be right to have one dog on its own. I don't like living on my own, so why should a dog like being on its own? Of course, Sally and I had each other, but a dog, no matter how much you love it, is not quite the same as another human being. It must be the same for dogs. In nature, wolves - the ancestors of dogs, I believe - operate in packs. Also there were times when I had to leave Sally at home on her own, especially to attend Church or Bible study.

So I contacted the nearest office of the National Canine Defence League. I am a member of the RSPCA, yet somehow I was led to the NCDL. They kindly gave me the name and telephone number of a family who were looking for a good home for a Jack Russell that, for some reason, they were unable to keep.

I wanted another small dog but I did not really want another Jack Russell. Sally was rather wilful! A good friend of mine, who also worked for the British Red Cross, told me "You can't train a Jack Russell" and I was inclined to agree with him.

However, I phoned them and we arranged a convenient time for Sally and I to meet the dog. I found the address and rang the door bell. The door was opened and Sally and I went in. Immediately there was trouble - the dog that we had come to see did not seem to appreciate Sally. So that was that.

I realised afterwards that we had made the tactical error of not arranging our meeting on neutral territory. If the dogs had met each other in a park and had a play together there, the outcome might have been different. The dog had simply been defending its own territory.

I contacted the NCDL again and told them what had happened. They suggested that I should visit their kennels, not far from Shrewsbury. Some days later, I had soon to go to The Royal Shrewsbury Hospital for a blood test, so I planned to visit the kennels afterwards.

When the day arrived, I took with me in the car the cat-basket in which Sally stayed while I was working at the Red Cross. I thought that it would keep the "new dog" under control during the journey home. Sally also came with me. After I had visited the Hospital and been given a "holiday" (a period of remission when no chemo-therapy is required), I set off for the Kennels.

Unfortunately, I arrived only a few minutes before their lunch hour. I had not even thought about the kennels being closed for lunch, otherwise I could have stopped for my own lunch somewhere. Nevertheless, they were extremely helpful and courteous to me and one of the staff showed me round the kennels.

That was a truly heart-breaking experience. Literally dozens of dogs, all in compartments rather like cages, most of them standing up on their hind legs, their front paws on the metal bars, barking as loudly as they could. I felt sure that the dogs knew exactly what was happening, just why I was there. Every one of them was saying "Please take me, please take me!".

Sally being female, I definitely wanted another female. I most certainly could not cope with a litter of puppies! As I have said before, I really wanted a smallish dog. On that day, they had very few small dogs ; if I remember correctly, not one of their small dogs was female.

I was taken to one compartment full of big dogs and shown one, a female. She was mostly white, with some small black spots and some large black patches - a Dalmatian cross. I thought that she seemed to be rather quiet and "retiring", not excitedly barking like the others.

The dog was brought out and I was offered the chance of walking her round a field accompanied by Sally, just to see how the two got on with each other. I accepted that offer immediately, collected Sally from the car and off we went round the field. I was told that the dog was called "Heather".

For Sally, it was "love at first sight". From the very first moment, she just adored Heather. Perhaps, to her, Heather was the mother or the sister that she had been missing. Heather seemed indifferent to Sally, not "anti", just indifferent. I must confess that I was not whole-hearted myself ; I was probably not yet reconciled to a big dog when I had come for a small one.

However, I thought : "Sally loves Heather, Heather is neutral towards Sally and she is certainly docile and easy to handle. Let's settle for that and be thankful." So I went to the office and said "Yes", even though Heather was somewhat bigger than the dog I had anticipated.

I learned that Heather had been admitted to the kennels when she was six months old and had been there for **twelve months**.

I was then almost overwhelmed by the legal side of the adoption. The would-be adopter has to agree to visits by an NCDL inspector, that if the dog can't be kept, it must be returned to the NCDL and, most important, that the dog will not be used for vivisection : all very necessary and laudable conditions. I signed on the dotted line and became the custodian of Heather. Can anyone **own** a dog any more than they can **own** a child?

After the legal formalities had been completed and I had given them a donation to the NCDL - necessary for an adoption - they very kindly provided me with a choke chain and lead, also a supply of the dog food to which she was accustomed. It reminded me of the armed forces' "unexpired portion of the day's rations", but I believe that the dogs had already been given all their ration of food for the day. The dogs there are fed on a dry complete dog food, which I had never seen before but which I now thoroughly recommend.

I must express my heartfelt gratitude to the staff of Roden Lane Farm for their courtesy and kindness to me, apart from all the fine work that they do, day after day, for the dogs in their care.

Then the three of us set off on our quite long journey home. We broke the journey at Montgomery Castle where both dogs were well behaved. Montgomery Castle was one of my wife's favourite places. It offers a magnificent view of the beauty of Mid-Wales.

Montgomery Castle

Then, just when we were driving into Newtown, Heather was violently sick. I was thankful that she had the sense and the consideration to do it on the rubber floor mat instead of on the passenger seat. It was impossible to stop until we reached the main town car park near Dolerw Park. Then, after I had removed the mess, I hugged Heather and said "It's all right, Heather, it doesn't matter!" Heather seemed to understand every word. From that moment on, we were **friends**. It was quite incredible.

The first week with Heather was **HORRENDOUS!**

Although the dogs at Roden do get out of their quarters for exercise, I imagine that they are not house-trained. Of necessity, they are locked up from late afternoon until the following morning. As Heather had been in Roden for twelve months, she was clearly accustomed to "unloading" in her living quarters. So I had to do some clearing up on the Tuesday morning, her first morning with me. I did my best to tell her that I was not too pleased, but obviously it was not her fault. She didn't know any better.

At 2 o'clock on Wednesday morning - in the middle of the night - I was woken up by Sally barking. Fearing an intruder, I got up and went to see what was wrong. There was more clearing up to do! Having done that, I thought "Well, at least all should be well in the morning." How wrong I was. When I got up, it was just as bad again.

When I took Heather and Sally out for a walk, it was very evident that Heather was not used to traffic. The NCDL kennels were some distance from the nearest road and that road was by no means a busy road. Once we were walking on the pavement under a railway bridge just when a train crossed the bridge above us. Heather was so frightened that I could hardly hold her.

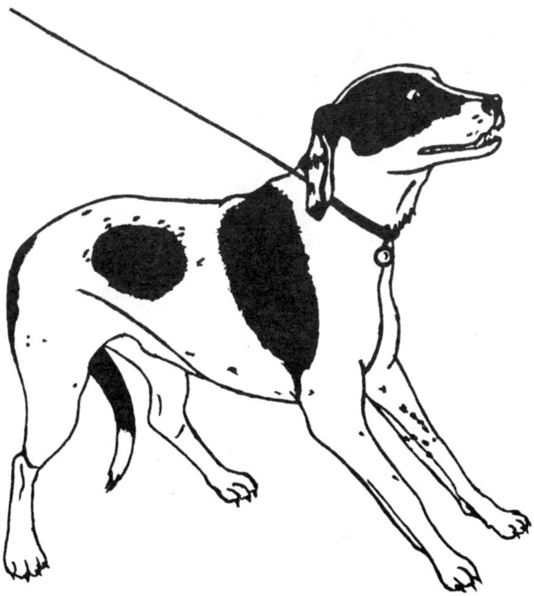

I was beginning to think that it was wrong to keep a dog in kennels for such a long time ; that after so many months in the kennels, a dog was so institutionalised that it was impossible for it ever to fit into an ordinary household again. I have heard the same thing said of human beings under somewhat similar circumstances.

I was not sure that I was giving Heather the correct quantity of food. I was also concerned that she appeared to be mute or dumb - she had never uttered a sound - so I phoned Roden Lane Farm to ask for help. I was reassured about the feeding and told that Heather was by no means mute, that she had a lovely deep bark.

Little by little, I won the house-training battle. I used a combination of reproach when Heather offended in the dogs bedroom together with a "reward" when she unloaded in a suitable place outdoors. Gradually also she became used to the traffic. Then one day I heard her bark - she has indeed got a lovely deep bark !

The first few days of silence must have been due to the trauma of being suddenly taken from the kennels. It must have been a terrific shock for her to be taken away from the staff who had cared for her and from her doggy friends : to be plunged into a different environment with a strange man and a lively, bossy little puppy. I felt so truly thankful that at last she was beginning to feel at home.

Outdoors and away from traffic, she was unbelievably well-behaved. The bond between Sally and Heather was now very strong, much stronger than the bond between Sally and myself. It almost made me feel left out. I was confident that, if I had one of them on the lead, I would have no problem with the other. Amazingly enough, I felt more confident letting Heather off the lead than letting Sally off the lead, even though Heather had only been with me a few days.

When you have only one dog, you get neurotic when it is out of sight, missing, even just for a minute or so. You are constantly seeking the dog because you feel that to lose your dog would shatter your life.

When you have two dogs, you are more relaxed. I don't mean that you become callous and uncaring, but losing one dog would not be quite such a disaster. You can then shift the responsibility onto the dogs to stay with you. You are not so anxious when they are some distance away from you. This is not only much easier and more pleasant for you but also more pleasant for the dogs. They have more freedom to explore and sniff and they are not constantly being nagged.

I was beginning to appreciate what a great dog and how faithful Heather was. I imagined that God had been chuckling and saying "You think that Sally is special. Son, you ain't seen nothing yet!" - except that I don't think that God would not be so ungrammatical.

You may be surprised, perhaps even shocked, by my talking about God chuckling. I firmly believe that God has a sense of humour. In fact, I claim that my belief is supported by the Word of God itself. No one can deny that most human beings have a sense of humour. Praise God that we have. How often we see the funny side of things when in adversity. Any one who was living during the 1939-45 war will testify to that. Am I allowed to ask you to reflect how many of our top comedians come from God's chosen race?

If we have a sense of humour, then so must the Lord,
" So God created man in His own image .... "

Genesis 1:27

I realised how wrong I had been about the wisdom or otherwise of keeping dogs so long in the kennels. Love and patience can always compensate for any length of time in the kennels. In fact, I believe that it is **because** Heather had been so long in the kennels that she is now so devoted and faithful to me.

I am not saying that she was not well-treated in the kennels. The very opposite - she expected every human being to love her and be kind to her, which proved how well-treated she had been. But after confinement in the kennels, even with devoted and loving care, life with me involving free walks in fields and chasing after a stick or a ball must have seemed like paradise to her. She was grateful for it.

I thought that I should have named the Jack Russell "Halle" and re-named the Dalmatian cross "Lujah" so that when I was calling them to me, instead of it being "Sally" "Heather" it would have been "Halle" "Lujah".

I did have a fright one day, only about ten days after I adopted Heather. Heather was off the lead, down by the river. Suddenly, she was running at full speed past me, clearly frightened out of her wits. All my calling was to no avail. I discovered that down by the river was an angler with a big black dog. It may have been that Heather gave the other dog a surprise so that it was stirred into action.

Whatever it was, I was terrified that I would never see Heather again, that - after so short a time with me - she would never be able to find her way home. After a long wide-ranging search, I dejectedly walked home intending to phone the police in the faint hope that they might be able to help.

Then, outside the house, I saw Heather coming towards me from the opposite direction. How she had got there, I have no idea. Soon I was hugging her, she was wagging her tail, I was nearly in tears, but tears of joy and relief. Once again, the Lord had answered my prayers.

Heather also seemed to have a sense of humour. At this time - before number 3 dog came onto the scene - we used to have many walks on less familiar territory. Frequently there were alternative paths to the same place. Heather had an uncanny knack of always finding an alternative path so that, when I was looking behind for her, there she was in front with a grin on her face.

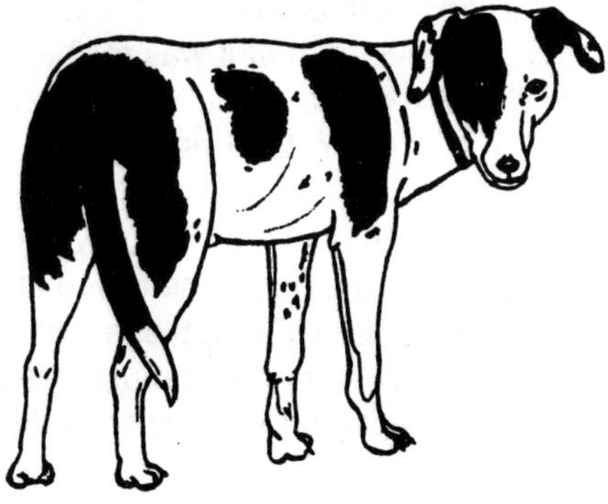

If, after drying her, I looked at Heather in a funny way, she would respond by nibbling my nose!

Heather is so devoted and faithful that I feel that it would be a sin for me to refuse her anything - provided that it was for her benefit and not to her detriment. Must not God feel the same way towards us if we are **truly** devoted and faithful to Him? And God never sins.

When I bought a bed for Sally, because she only needed a very small one, the difference in price between a plastic hard bed and a nylon fur soft one was so small that I treated her to a soft one. When I bought Heather's much larger one, the price difference was much greater so I bought a less expensive hard bed. After all, in the kennels she might well have had to lie on concrete.

Unfortunately, when I returned home after leaving them on their own, I almost invariably found Heather lying **on** the small soft bed - she was too big to lie **in** it - and little Sally was in the big hard bed.

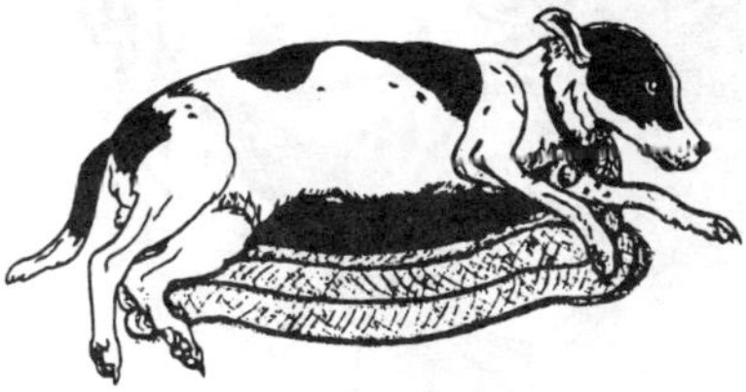

Call me a softy if you like, but I thought "I don't want a confrontation over this ; Heather deserves better than that".

So I bought Heather a big soft bed. She was in the car when I collected it and I am sure that she knew what was happening. When I put it into their bedroom, Heather got into it and didn't come out of it for three hours. She was so thrilled and pleased that it filled me with joy as well.

Of course, this didn't mean that each of them now slept in their own bed. Most of the time they slept together in the big bed. But that in itself gave me great joy.

God too must rejoice and enjoy seeing us when we are at peace with each other and enjoying each other's company. He must also be sad - and cross - when there is tension or fighting between us, just as I am when there is tension or fighting between my dogs, thankfully a very rare occasion.

I am sure that my love for them breeds love between them just as God's infinite love for us should breed love between His children.

You may well imagine that I now amended my recommendation to people left on their own and to some people with health problems to "Get a dog! Better still, get two dogs!". I also decided that, if I could possibly avoid it, I would never again have one dog on its own.

Sally and Heather enjoyed having a tug-of-war over a rubber bone or a pentagonal rubber ring. It was interesting to see that, at first, Sally used to shake and twist her end - as though shaking a rat - whereas Heather relied on sheer power, superior strength or brute force. But soon Heather cottoned on to this and started shaking and twisting her end as well.

Heather likes playing with a ball, but she doesn't want me to throw it for her to fetch. She prefers to keep it in her mouth, just outside my grasp, and make me chase her!

Both Sally and Heather soon began to enjoy swimming in the river. At first, Heather was very wary of the river. I imagine that she had never seen a river before, let alone thought of going into one. Adventurous little Sally was the first to swim, encouraged by a ball or a stick - I forget which - but she preferred to swim close to the river bank. Then Heather was swimming as well.

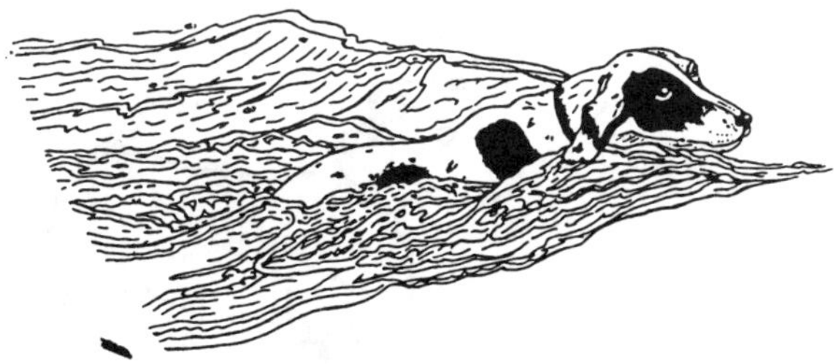

Heather enjoyed swimming to fetch a ball, she did bring It back to me, dropping it in the water by the river bank so that I could **just** reach it!

We humans think how clever we are, but I can remember how long it took me to learn to swim. Even after many months of effort, I would not call myself a good swimmer. When dogs decide that they want to swim, they just go in and swim! Just as simple as that.

There was a particularly good swimming place further up the river than I usually took them, the river was both broad and deep. Heather would not only swim for a stick but just swim round and round for the sheer joy of it. I believe that she could also smell something interesting on the other bank - perhaps sheep or horses.

It dawned on me then just how much trust I had in Heather. If she had swum across and climbed up the other bank and declined to come back, I should have been in a real predicament!

It was also easy to stir Heather into action when Sally had got a ball, some other doggy toy or a piece of stick. All I had to do was call to her "Sally's got it!" and there would be a fast, mad chase.

At one time, we used to walk down a very narrow path near the river. It had become overgrown by the hedges, many of which were prickly. No one seemed to be controlling the hedges, so one day, rightly or wrongly, I decided to be a "Boy Scout". I took some pruning shears with me in a bag and set to work lopping off the shoots overhanging the path.

Unfortunately, I was so immersed in my day's good turn that I stumbled over a metal grate at the side of the path. I found to my utter horror that under the grate there was a wasps' nest and they did not appreciate being disturbed. I received two quite serious stings and, despite my efforts to get the two dogs out of danger as quickly as possible, Heather was definitely stung and Sally may have been also.

I avoided that path for a couple of months, making a detour through a housing estate with the dogs on leads. I then thought that it should be safe to use it again but Heather thought differently. There was no way by which I could get Heather down that path if she didn't want to go. She may not be an elephant but she certainly has a long memory.

At this time, I was still working for the Red Cross. Obviously, I could not take two dogs with me to the office, not when one was as big as Heather. So I had to restrict the time I gave to the Red Cross. I can see now that this was the first step in God's plan to extract me from the Red Cross because He had other work for me to do.

I still had to attend committee meetings in Llandrindod Wells, but - once again - the Lord's provision was perfect. Jill, a good friend of mine, had been the mainstay and my colleague in the Mid-Wales Regional office of the Luis Palau "Tell Wales" mission. She lived half-way between Newtown and Llandrindod Wells, so, provided that she was not otherwise committed, Jill was always willing - and happy - to look after my two dogs when I went to a meeting.

I was advised by a friend that it was potentially dangerous - if not illegal - to have two unrestrained dogs in the car with me. It is impossible to control a car and two dogs at the same time. Even a little dog like Sally could cause an accident if she exploded into a bark at the sight of another dog or - worse still - her arch enemy, a ***motor bike*** !

So I decided that I would have to change my Regata saloon for a hatchback, in which the dogs could be safe and sound behind a dog guard. My conscience was troubled by the expense involved. I tried to salve my conscience by giving my old car to Ichthus Motor Mission. Ichthus operate a car loan service to assist missionaries on furlough in the U.K.

Ichthus told me that the handing over to them of my Regata could not have been more timely. Recently, the demand for cars by missionaries had surpassed their ability to supply them. Sorrowfully, they had been compelled to say "No" to requests for cars. They welcomed my car with open arms and thanksgiving to the Lord. As always, His timing was perfect - and my conscience was no longer troubled.

About a month or so after I adopted Heather, I was led to visit my G.P. again. After the customary greetings, I said "I've come to save the N.H.S. some money. I'm out in the fresh air more than two hours a day, walking about three miles a day. If I want to climb up a river bank, provided that my boots will grip, I go straight up it. Do I need to be on beta blockers?"

After a few minutes check-up, I was told "No. Take it easy for the first week to let your system get accustomed to the change, but I don't think that you will have any problems." I thanked the G.P. and went on my way rejoicing.

Praise the Lord !

Chapter 3 LADY

After my friends had recovered from the shock of my adoption of a second dog, one or two of them asked me "Are you having any more?". "NO WAY!" I said very firmly, "I've only got TWO hands."

Once again, God was to prove me wrong. No, I don't mean that I've got three hands, but that I **was** going to have another dog.

Sally was thoroughly enjoying being with Heather and getting lots of fun and exercise playing with her. She certainly pestered me less to play with her. But Heather did not get the exercise that she required because Sally is so much smaller than she is.

Then, one Saturday afternoon when we were in Dolerw Park, Sally was off on her own having a good sniff around - to get the latest news of what had been happening there. Heather was having a wonderful time playing and racing with a lovely black-and-white collie. I was chatting to the Collie's owner - or should I say keeper.

There is a great camaraderie, a great fellowship, between dog lovers. We are happy to spend hours - well minutes - talking about our dogs, how we acquired them, what they've been doing. I think that I have now more dog-lover friends than any other friends.

Is there such camaraderie between Christians? Are we equally willing, let alone eager, to spend time talking to each other about what God has been doing for us? Of course, it's not as easy to recognise a Christian as it is to recognise a dog lover. I'm not suggesting that we should all wear dog-collars (white ones not leather ones). But perhaps we should all wear a badge, such as a fish, to show where we stand and so that we **can** recognise each other easily.

I had remarked to the lady with the collie what a lovely dog she had. The lady informed me that, due to circumstances, she was unable to keep the collie and that she was looking for a good home for her. It was a clear invitation to adopt her.

As I have mentioned earlier, I had no intention whatsoever of having a third dog, but somehow I began to wonder. I made a note of the lady's telephone number and continued with our walk.

I considered the matter very carefully, seeking the Lord's will. I decided to do nothing for one week and then make contact. If, after that time, the collie was still there and had not been adopted by anyone else, then I would have it - it must be God's will that I should do so.

The week passed and I made contact - the collie still needed a home. So that was that. I went to the lady's home and she very kindly came with me, Heather and Sally, for a walk round Dolerw Park. The dogs became good friends and then the lady left the collie "Lady" on the lead with me.

At first, Lady wanted to follow her former keeper but then somehow she seemed to sense and accept the situation. I had no trouble whatsoever in leading her to the car. Dogs have more sense, intuition, intelligence - call it what you like - than most people attribute to them.

Sally was not at all impressed with the idea of Lady being lifted into the boot of **her** car. However, it was only a short journey home and then I was able to make sure that there was no trouble between Sally and Lady.

Very quickly, Sally accepted the fact that she now had another "sister" and really appreciated having another playmate. How often do we initially react ungratefully to something which, in the long run, proves to be a blessing?

Lady was already house-trained and she would came to me when I called her. I could let her off the lead - in a suitable place - straight away and know that she would come back to me. She settled into the household incredibly quickly.

I had to learn to cope with the leads of three dogs in two hands. I decided to have Sally and Heather together on my left, their leads in my left hand, and Lady on my right, her lead in my right hand. I found to my amazement that Sally and Heather were easier to control now than they had been with one lead in each hand. It was as though they had decided that they had to set an example to this lively young puppy!

Lady is a dreadful "puller" and very strong, but thanks to a tip from another dog-lover, I purchased a "Haltie" which fits over the head and gives more control than the collar. That certainly solved the problem, in fact it is so effective that I now realise that Heather pulls as well, though I don't intend to buy her a Haltie. (Sorry if this sounds like a commercial break.)

There was now even more fun for the dogs playing together and for me watching them. Outdoors, it was mostly Heather and Lady playing together. Indoors, it was mostly Sally and Lady playing together. Often all three of them would have a "rough and tumble" or a tug-of-war. If you can get all three dogs after the same toy or the same piece of stick, then you are really winning. It is wonderful to see them playing together and see how gently the bigger dogs use their paws to hold or push little Sally.

They like to play and have a race with other dogs - each dog wants to find out if it can beat the other - but, if there are no other dogs about, they can always have fun within the family.

When a dog meets a stranger dog, there is always a lot of standing or lying and watching, weighing the other one up, then slowly approaching and giving each other a good sniff round before they start playing or chasing.

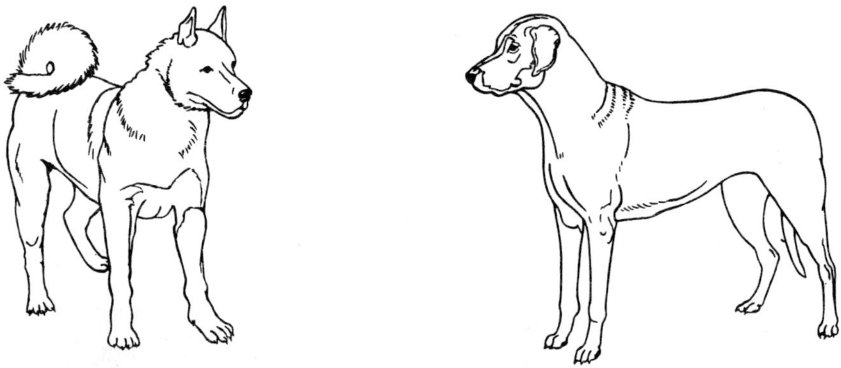

Within the family, no time is wasted on these preliminary formalities. If they feel like playing, they just get on with it. Sometimes when Lady feels like it, she will just run full speed at one of the others whether the other likes it or expects it or not!

Lady loves to chase anything, the faster the better, birds being ideal. At one time of the year, there were swifts in the park. That gave rise to some two-way fun. Just as much as Lady liked to chase them, the swifts equally enjoyed "buzzing" her - flying fast and low over her - to tease her and urge her on to greater efforts ! It was equally fun for me just watching.

Lady is very keen on fetching a ball. She does not bring it right back to me so that I can take it from her mouth, but she brings it fairly close, drops it and stands over it. She doesn't just want - and expect - to be taken for a walk, she expects me to throw a ball for her as well. The first evening after "the clocks went back" she expected me to throw the ball for her when it was so dark that I could scarcely see Lady herself never mind a ball.

I was seriously asthmatic when I was at school - I was often called "Wheezy Anna" after a pop song of the day, because I could be heard wheezing from the other side of the road. So I didn't do much P.E. and never developed a good over-arm throw.

I have to throw under-arm, aiming at an angle of 45 degrees in order to achieve the maximum range. However, this suits Lady very well because it gives her just sufficient time to be able to catch the ball on its first rebound from the ground. I would say that her success rate is about 80%. She sometimes catches the ball when it is four feet in the air.

She enjoys swimming for a ball even more than Heather does. Given the slightest opportunity, she will "hog" Heather's "go". To give Heather a chance, I have to hold Lady by the collar while throwing the ball for Heather. However, because Lady can be relied on to bring the ball right up the river bank, I usually release her when Heather has nearly reached the bank.

On one occasion, for some reason known only to themselves, both Heather and Lady suddenly "switched off" leaving the ball in the river out of my reach. They completely ignored my pleas "Fetch the ball! Fetch the ball!"

However, little Sally, who had not been involved in the ball-fetching, immediately got the message. She went into the river and made two or three valiant attempts to get the ball. Unfortunately, the ball was larger than her open jaws, so that every time she grabbed for the ball, she simply pushed it further away.

I thought "Another ball down the drain - or rather down the river", climbed up the river bank and started to walk away.

I hadn't walked many yards when good old Sally came trotting up, the ball in her mouth, as proud as proud could be. You can imagine the hearty welcome which she received. I can only conclude that Sally managed to push the ball against a stone in the river and so get a grip on it. Like all terriers, she has "stickability" - she never gives up.

The time came for Lady to be in season. This was by no means as easy as it had been with Sally. Free-ranging male dogs seemed to appear from every direction. Sometimes, if there was only one dog on the prowl, I thought that it was fairer to put the dog on the lead and let Lady enjoy herself rather than condemn Lady to being on the lead.

I thought that it was safe to give Lady exercise swimming for a ball in the river, while I stood guard on the bank. To give her as much exercise as possible, I threw the ball as far as I could. But, one day, I threw it too far so that, after getting the ball, Lady decided that it was closer to the **other** bank - and that's where she went !

A few months after Lady had been in season, I had her spayed. As I have said earlier, I could not cope with puppies. I had already had Sally spayed. I just thought that it was the obvious thing to do. It was only when, a week later, there was a lot of public discussion about a different ethical issue, that it occurred to me that spaying Lady might not have been God's will. How often do we take decisions for granted without seeking guidance from the Lord?

I must confess that I preferred it to be fine when I took the dogs out. It is a bit of a chore to dry three dogs with a towel - or sometimes two towels. Because Sally is so small, the most convenient way to dry her is for me to sit at the bottom of the stairs and put Sally on my lap like a baby being changed.

The other dogs then sit on the stairs above me. There seems to be a hierarchy - a competition to be furthest up the stairs. Fair enough unless there is someone or something outside. I can assure you that the effect of a dog's loud bark, only one inch from your left ear, is not pleasant!

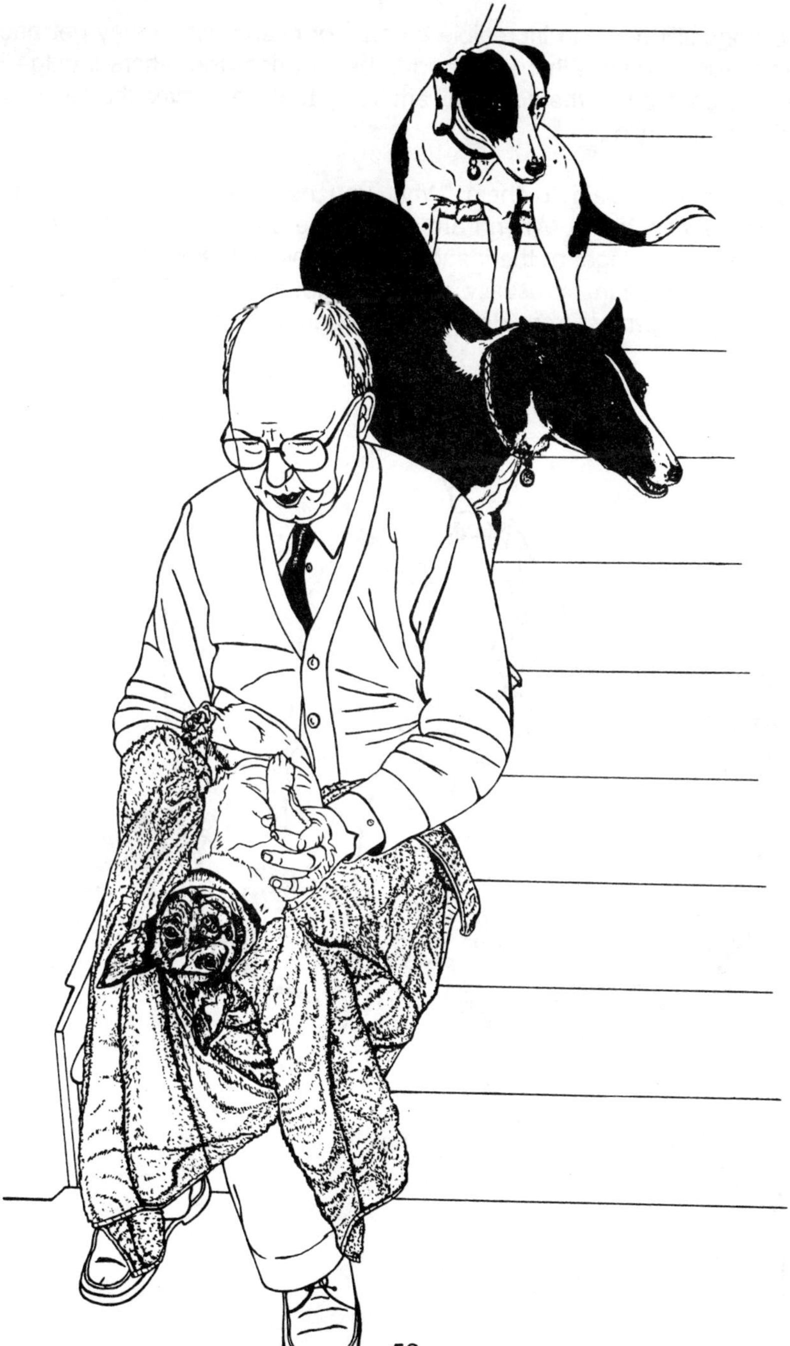

The dogs still have an incredible amount of energy when they get back home from a walk. When one dog is being dried, the others indulge in nibbling each other, the dog that I am trying to dry and even the hand that is doing the drying.

One morning, I said to them "What you need is discipline!". So that became a new game. When I am drying one dog, I tell the others to sit down, wag my finger at them and say "Discipline! Discipline!".
Amazingly enough, it usually works, although there is often a loud "rumbling" of protest from Heather when I am drying Lady.

Chapter 4 Questions and Answers

Don't you ever think that it would be better if the money that the dogs cost were given to the Third World ?

Yes, I do think about that. I learned about stewardship the hard way when my wife died and I was left with the responsibility of disposing of all her property. I sometimes think that the word "stewardship" isn't strong enough, even though the scriptures speak of us being stewards. I feel that I am **responsible** to God for all the things that He has given me, including any talents which I may have.

But I accept - and I say this with all reverence and humility - that God knows what He is doing. His judgement must be best and that the work that He wants me to do and that He is enabling to do by the provision of my dogs must justify the money which cannot be sent to the Third World.

Do you have a favourite ?

I try hard to be even-handed in my dealings with my dogs. They are all quite different in character which makes being with them so much more interesting and more fun. They all have their own good points and their own weaknesses.

Sally is full of fun - sometimes mischief - and probably the most intelligent, but she is sometimes too independent. At home, she is almost always the centre of activity. Her face is so expressive, it shows when she is full of fun and mischief. Heather is faithful, gentle and docile, but perhaps too self-effacing. Lady is lively, full of energy but perhaps slightly more aloof than the others.

Sally has always come onto my lap during the evening. After a few weeks, Lady decided that she wanted to do the same. I couldn't cope with Heather on my lap as well - Lady is heavy enough - so I made a deal with Heather. She stays on the rug or in a dog-bed during the evening but, at night, she is allowed to sleep in her bed in my bedroom.

Heather is full of love. First thing each morning, when Heather wakes up, if she sees that I am awake, she comes straight across to me and licks my face. Not because she wants to go out or because she wants food, but just to say "Hello, it's good to be with you. I love you!". Then she very contentedly goes back into her bed and usually goes to sleep again.

When **we** wake up, do we go straight to God, metaphorically lick His face and say "Hello, Father, it's good to be with You. I love You"?

Lady is full of energy, she never walks anywhere, she always runs. She abounds with the joy of being alive, all too frequently expressed by jumping and barking.

How do you react to Heather's early morning greetings?

It fills me with love for her and **PRAISE and THANKSGIVING to the LORD** for His goodness to me. Of course, I know that we shouldn't **need** a visual reminder to make us grateful to God for all that He has done for us - especially Jesus and our salvation.

I sometimes wonder if Heather knows just how much I love her - even though I occasionally have to rebuke her. I am sure that she does. Do we know just how much God loves us - even though He frequently has to discipline us?

But which would you choose if you could only keep one of them?

I think that it would have to be Heather. The others could probably survive without me but Heather would be completely shattered. I probably love her the most because she loves me more than the others do.

I often wonder about the phrase *The disciple whom Jesus loved*. It almost implies that Jesus did not love the other disciples and yet we know that He did.

Love one another as I have loved you

Does the phrase mean that Jesus loved John especially because John **loved** Jesus especially - more than the other disciples?

I understand that every group of dogs has a pack leader. Who is the pack leader amongst your dogs?

I'm not sure. I believe that the only way to find out for certain would be to put just one bowl of food down and see what happened. Actually, I feed and dry them in the order in which they arrived - Sally, Heather, Lady. But I would not **want** to see what happened. I am most careful that they each have their own bowl and eat separately.

I think that the pack leader is probably Sally and the "pecking order" Sally, Lady, Heather. That does not mean that Heather is any the less in my eyes, far from it.

I am sure that the same applies to human beings. Those who are great in their own eyes and perhaps even in the eyes of other people may well be the smallest in God's eyes.

Blessed are the meek, for they will inherit the earth."

Matthew 5:5

Do they ever disappoint you?

Very rarely, but it has happened. Once when I had parked the car in the main car park, I set off walking westward on the South side of the river. Sally was lagging behind, enjoying a good sniff, as she liked to do. Heather and Lady were with me. I was confident that Sally would soon catch up with us.

When, after a while, she did not appear, I got worried and started to look for her. When I couldn't see her anywhere, I got quite frantic yet Heather and Lady seemed to be quite indifferent that Sally was lost. So I felt rather angry with them, probably more so than with the wayward one herself.

Won't God be frantic and equally angry - or even angrier - at our indifference when our fellow human beings are lost for all eternity?

Do you ever "fall out" with them?

I am thankful to say very rarely. But I remember that once even Heather offended by eating some dirt, the temptation to which they seem most likely to fall. I had admonished her and washed her mouth out but she knew by my voice that she was still in my bad books.

She came to me, sat up and begged - not for food, or to go out, but clearly for forgiveness and reconciliation.

Needless to say, she was forgiven immediately and I loved her even more than before : we were friends again. I can't remain cross with a repentant sinner. I found that too when I was a teacher.

When we sin against God, do we "sit up and beg" for forgiveness and reconciliation? If we are truly repentant and beg for mercy, how could the Lord not forgive us when He is love personified?

Do your dogs often get injured or sick?

I truly thank God that they don't. They seem to be quite impervious to pain inflicted on them in play when they are bitten, probably "nibbled" is more fitting, on their legs or their necks. But the pads of their paws seem to be very sensitive to pain, Lady in particular.

Sometimes in the Park, she will come up to me holding one paw with a woeful look on her face.

But the look is not just woeful, it is also expectant. She expects me to be able to put it right. I don't mean "expects" in the sense of "takes for granted", but "expects" in the sense of "certainty, complete confidence, absolute faith".

Do we have such certainty, complete confidence, absolute faith, when we go to the Lord and ask for His help? Clearly, we should have. If a dog can have such faith in a mere mortal, surely we should have the same faith in our eternal God?

As I write this, Lady has a damaged pad on her right back paw. When my car was "poorly", I used to say that it made me poorly as well. But that was sheer selfishness - it was inconvenient for me when I was deprived of the advantages of a car. But when one of the dogs is not 100% fit, I feel sad as well, not just out of sympathy but true empathy.

How do you cope with three dogs in the Park?

Coping with three dogs is easy, provided that they are only playing with one toy or ball. But if, between them, they have two toys or balls, it is difficult. It isn't a question of watching the dogs, it's a question of keeping track of the toys. Losing more than one a week gets a bit expensive.

How about at home in the bungalow?

Well, it's not advisable to have them on your lap when drinking coffee or to put a mug of coffee on a low coffee table.

I was once drinking coffee when Sally and Lady were lying peacefully on my lap. Unfortunately, something or someone outside caused a minor "explosion" as they leapt off my knees to bark at the intruder - just happening to spill coffee all over me.

It's all quite common when you are sitting quietly to have a little Jack Russell dash past you at full speed with the two bigger dogs in hot pursuit. If the coffee table just happens to be in the way, "Tough!".

In the bungalow, Sally has the advantage. She can dive under furniture - including my bed - and behind the settee, where the others can't follow. She loves to tease them by sticking her head out from one end of the settee to lure them into dashing there, running along behind the settee and then sticking her head out from the other end.

I have given them a rubber bone and I can always stir them into playful activity by asking "Where's the bone? Where's the bone?".

Do you have any special problems with them?

I think probably most are due to the thoughtlessness of some people, such as smashing bottles and leaving broken glass on paths and on the grass in the park, where dogs can tread on it and seriously damage their paws.

Fireworks are another problem. I am thankful that Sally and Lady are not frightened by fireworks, I worry a little that if Sally saw one she might sniff at it and try to eat it. But Heather is really scared. Her tail goes down right between her legs and she visibly shivers.

At such times, she likes the security of home or the boot of our car. Outside those, she prefers to be on the lead. The lead offers no protection against the noise or the firework, yet it gives her security. Do we feel the same security when the Lord is leading us?

If we must have fireworks, it would help if they were confined to one special evening, presumably the fifth of November, but were not exploded at any time on any other day. We could then make sure that our dogs - and other pets - were safely at home. But I must get off my hobby-horse and back to the dogs!

Similarly, Heather is frightened by thunder and lightning. Early one morning I saw her shivering, shaking with fear. it was quite some time before I heard the thunder that she had been hearing. I hugged her to try to console her, saying "Don't worry, Heather, I am with you!"
Isn't that just what God says to us?

Do not be afraid, for I am with you;

Isaiah 43:5

Are you going to adopt any more dogs?

Only the Lord knows the answer to that one.

Have you any other comments?

Yes. At the time of writing, I have been on "holiday" (remission, free from chemo-therapy) for more than **two years**, by far the longest period of remission that I have enjoyed since my CLL was first diagnosed.

PRAISE THE LORD !

Praise the Lord, O my soul ;
all my inmost being, praise his holy name.

Praise the Lord, O my soul,
and forget not all his benefits -

who forgives all your sins
and heals all your diseases,

who redeems you from the pit
and crowns you with love and compassion

who satisfies your desires with good things
so that your youth is renewed like the eagle's.

Psalm 103 1-5

Chapter 5 Background

At the time of his retirement at the end of December 1985, Alick Hartley was Senior Teacher in charge of Examinations at Westcliff High School for Girls, Essex. His wife, Kathleen, was also teaching at another school in Essex.

Alick had for some years felt called to teach overseas but Kathleen felt unable to do so while her elderly mother was still alive. After the death of Kathleen's mother as the result of a tragic house fire in March 1984, they started pushing at several doors to see if one opened, but none did.

During their summer holiday in 1985, they went to India to see if they could cope with the climate, the conditions and the altitude - roughly 11,500 feet above mean sea level - in order to help in a Mission school in Leh, Ladakh in the Himalayas.

The climate, conditions and altitude proved to be no obstacles. In fact, Alick enjoyed several games of Badminton at that altitude, on an improvised court in the school playground. He even had the satisfaction of seeing his Ladakhi opponent take off his sweater - something that Ladakhis rarely do, even when Europeans are in shirt sleeves!

However, at that time, it was difficult to get permits to work in India. There were also problems in the administration of the school itself.

While in India, due to the heat and different food, Alick lost a lot of weight. He expected to put it on again after their return to England. He found that he had little appetite and, instead of gaining weight, he continued to lose weight.

Being a mathematician, he easily calculated that if his weight loss continued at the same rate, he would have completely disappeared before the end of two years. He resolved to see his G.P. as soon as he had time, after he had retired and finished marking his quota of winter overseas G.C.E. papers.

He was also sweating profusely at night in bed. So, by reading some home doctor book, he reduced the possible causes to two, one of them being leukaemia. It was not therefore such a great shock when, after a blood test, a barium X-ray and a bone marrow test in early 1986, he was diagnosed as having CLL (chronic lymphatic leukaemia).

He was immediately put on a course of chemo-therapy. The change was dramatic. To him, the improvement produced by a few little tablets was little short of a miracle.

Alick discovered that he felt much healthier in the country, away from the Southend area. A long chain of events - which can now only be interpreted as God's hand at work - led Alick and Kath to move to Newtown in Mid-Wales at August Bank Holiday in 1986.

Kath had been granted early retirement but had to work until the end of the year, one term after they moved to Wales. Unfortunately, Kath was only able to travel over to Newtown for one weekend before she was very ill and was shortly diagnosed as having cancer. She had to have a hysterectomy and then chemo-therapy.

Kath was blessed by being given the use of a small flat by a good friend of hers until she was able to secure an even tinier flat of her own as a base in Southend, where she was having the chemo-therapy. Alick travelled over from Wales as often as possible and was able to stay with Kath in the flat.

Kath was not fit to travel until spring of the following year, when she was able to make short visits to Wales between doses of chemo-therapy. She seemed to be making an excellent recovery and, during the summer, was able to enjoy the beauty of Mid-Wales, in particular the green hills, the many sheep and the coast at Aberdovey.

But that recovery was not to last. From September onwards, she began to deteriorate and died in Southend General Hospital towards the end of January 1988.

Alick was absolutely devastated. With Kath at his side, he had always felt that together they could cope with anything, endure anything. Their trip to India had not been a bed of roses but together - and with encouragement from the Lord - they had coped. If called to do so, they had been eager to go back again for much longer service.

Left on his own, Alick felt utterly helpless, that his life was over as well. Being ten years older than his wife, he had never even contemplated that Kath might die before him.

Nevertheless, he was grateful to God that they had been led to move to Wales while they both still thought that Kath was healthy ; grateful that Kath had enjoyed at least a few months in the beauty of Mid-Wales before she was called to be with her Lord.

Alick could not have afforded to stay in the house in which they had lived in Leigh-on-Sea, yet he could not have faced the trauma of moving on his own. The Lord's timing eliminated that dilemma. God had also provided him with many committed Christian friends in Wales.

He was still keen to write some Mathematics and Statistics textbooks, but writing is a very solitary and lonely occupation. It is all right if there is someone else in the room, or even in the house, with whom to have coffee, an occasional chat, meals and the recreational part of the day. But, if there is no one sharing your house, it is the very last occupation for someone recently bereaved.

Soon the Lord gave him other work to do, Alick had offered his services - on the accounts side - to a few charitable organisations. His offer was accepted by the Red Cross. As a result of the recommendation of a Christian friend, he was also invited to assist in the Mid-Wales region of the Luis Palau "Tell Wales" Mission.

He suddenly became fully occupied from Monday to Friday, even though the weekends were still a void. The Lord seemed to be behind both projects ; it was amazing - or should I say **providential** - how the two so different activities helped each other.

At the Red Cross, he learned how to use PC File, a simple but very efficient computer database. This new knowledge proved to be invaluable in his work for "Tell Wales".

"Tell Wales" employed a centralised accounts system - all accounting and payments were handled at their Headquarters. The Powys Branch of the British Red Cross was just on the verge of centralising their accounts. Experience gained from "Tell Wales" was equally invaluable to him in his work for the Red Cross.

But a full day, his time divided between two offices, led him to have lunch in town, a regular diet of fish and chips. This may well have led to his angina, which was first diagnosed the very day after the "Tell Wales" National Rally at Cardiff Arms Park, the climax of the mission. He was then put onto Beta blockers.

After the completion of his work for "Tell Wales", he continued to work for the Red Cross ...... and "that's where we came in" - as people used to say in the days of continuous cinema shows.

Alick is now a director of **GWELFRYN PUBLICATIONS LIMITED**, publishers of Christian and Educational books. God has provided him with three colleagues in his publishing work, all members of Newtown Pentecostal Church. Alick himself is a member of Newtown Evangelical Church.

Alick is also a director of **APEX BUSINESS CENTRE (NEWTOWN) LIMITED**, which company uses the very considerable computer expertise acquired in the course of publishing to supply and assist other people who may be new to the use of computers.

In 1992, Alick instigated the formation of **GLOBAL BOOK SUPPORT**, a charity which organises the free distribution throughout the world of a limited range of Christian and Educational books. The Trustees feel that they are particularly called to assist Evangelistic work, Hospital Chaplains, Missionaries, Prison Chaplains, Schools and Youth Organisations. Communications and donations should be addressed to :

The Trustees, GLOBAL BOOK SUPPORT, 18d High Street, NEWTOWN, Powys SY16 2NP, United Kingdom.

Acknowledgements

The author wishes to offer his very sincere thanks to -

(a) the student who brought Sally to his door

(b) the National Canine Defence League for all their good work

(c) the staff of Roden Lane Farm for all their courtesy and kindness to humans as well as dogs

(d) the many dog-loving friends that he has met during the last few months

(e) the staff of Hafren Veterinary Surgery for their loving care of his "family"

(f) the staff of the Haematology Departments at Southend General Hospital and the Royal Shrewsbury Hospital for their devoted care

(g) the various organisations who undertake research into Leukaemia and Cancer

(h) his many friends for reading the drafts of this book and offering helpful suggestions

(i) Wendy Howard for providing such excellent illustrations

(j) Rachel Hewitt for "tying the book together".

Other books published by GWELFRYN PUBLICATIONS LTD

Bible-based puzzle books

(a)	**"SEARCH THE WORD"** A half-completed specimen puzzle is given on page 81	57 puzzles	£1.00
(b)	**"QUOTATION QUIZ"** A specimen page is given on page 82	358 quotations	£1.00
(c)	**"BURIED TREASURE"** A half-completed specimen puzzle is given on page 83	38 puzzles	£1.00
(d)	**"LINKS WITHIN THE WORD"** A half-completed specimen puzzle is given on page 84	19 puzzles	£1.00
(e)	**"MORE LINKS WITHIN THE WORD"** A half-completed specimen puzzle is given on page 85	23 puzzles	£1.00
(f)	**"CROSSED KEYS"** A half-completed specimen puzzle is given on page 86	20 puzzles	£1.00
(g)	**"TRYSOR CUDD"** (Welsh) A completed example is given on page 87	36 puzzles	£1.50

Books to assist the teaching/learning of basic English vocabulary

(a)	**"PICSEARCH"** A half-completed specimen puzzle is given on page 88	20 puzzles	£1.65
(b)	**"CROSSPICS"** A completed part of a puzzle is given on page 89	15 puzzles each with 24 clues	£1.00

Other educational books

(a) **"CAN I HELP YOU?"** Alick Hartley, B.Sc. £1.00
A 64-page easy-to-read introduction to the uses of computers.

(b) **"BASIC ACCOUNTS FOR THE CHURCH TREASURER"**
The principles of elementary accounts. £2.00

(c) **"SIMPLIFIED ACCOUNTS FOR THE CHARITY TREASURER"**
The principles of elementary accounts. £2.00

(d) **"STEP-BY-STEP GUIDE FOR THE HONORARY TREASURER"**
The principles of elementary accounts for the treasurers of societies or clubs. £2.00

(e) **"BASIC STATISTICS"** Alick Hartley, B.Sc. £4.50

(f) **"BASIC STATISTICS - TEACHERS GUIDE"** £1.00

(g) **"ADDITIONAL STATISTICS"** Alick Hartley, B.Sc. £4.50

(h) **"ADDITIONAL STATISTICS - TEACHERS GUIDE"** £1.00

A half-completed puzzle from "SEARCH THE WORD"

THINGS OF WHICH THERE IS ONLY ONE (8)

B	O	D	Y	U	G	L
F	A	T	H	E	R	O
D	L	P	H	H	W	R
C	T	T	T	O	Z	D
X	T	I	R	I	P	S
A	A	W	C	Q	S	E
F	X	G	O	D	I	M

A specimen page from "QUOTATION QUIZ"

66 *But if you do not forgive men their sins...* (7)

67 *But many who are first will be last...* (8)

68 *But now in Christ Jesus you who once were far away...* (9)

69 *But now that you have been set free from sin and have become slaves to God...* (13)

70 **But seek first his kingdom and his righteousness...** (11)

71 **But thanks be to God! He gives us the victory...** (5)

72 But when you pray, go into your room... (11)

73 But you are a chosen people, a royal priesthood, a holy nation, **a** people belonging to God... (18)

74 By their fruit you will recognise them... (10)

75 **Carry each other's burdens, and in this way...** (7)

76 **Cast your cares on the LORD and he will sustain you...** (7)

77 **Come to me, all you who are weary and burdened...** (6)

78 **Commit to the LORD whatever you do...** (5)

79 *Consider how the lilies grow. They do not labour or spin. Yet I tell you...* (13)

80 *Delight yourself in the LORD...* (10)

81 *Do everything without complaining or arguing, so that you may become blameless and pure...* (20)

82 Do not be anxious about anything, but in everything, by prayer and petition... (7)

A half-completed specimen puzzle from "BURIED TREASURE"

<u>SOAPSTONE</u> (11 words)

D	E	S	S	E	L	B
R	S	E	Y	S	H	K
J	G	E	P	P	A	T
A	H	K	E	U	E	R
T	E	J	D	X	R	A
L	L	I	W	O	A	E
A	N	P	F	N	G	H

→ → ....

← ← (2) BLESSED , WILL ....

↓ ↓ ....

↑ ↑ (2) ARE , HEART ....

↘ ↘ (2) SEE , PURE ....

↖ ↖ (2)..

↗ ↗ (2)..

↙ ↙ (1)..

BLESSED ARE ☐☐☐ PURE ☐☐

HEART ☐☐☐ ☐☐☐☐ WILL SEE

☐☐☐

A half-completed specimen puzzle from "LINKS WITHIN THE WORD"

THINGS THAT LOVE IS (6)

1 Corinthians 13:4 1 Corinthians 13:7

A half-completed puzzle from "MORE LINKS WITHIN THE WORD"

THINGS THAT LOVE IS NOT (7)

1 Corinthians 13:4
1 Corinthians 13:5
1 Corinthians 13:8

A half-completed specimen puzzle from "CROSSED KEYS"

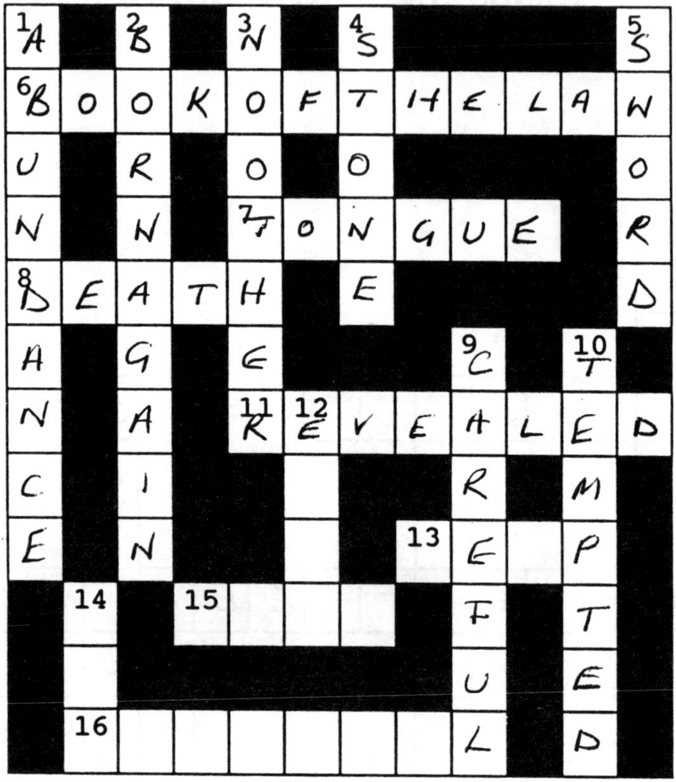

ACROSS

6. Joshua 1:8 (4,2,3,3)
7. 1 Corinthians 14:13 (6)
8. 1 Corinthians 15:55 (5)
11. Deuteronomy 29:29 (8)
13. Psalm 46:1 (4)
15. Matthew 5:41 (4)
16. Matthew 5:7 (8)

DOWN

1. Matthew 25:29 (9)
2. John 3:7 (4,5)
3. Exodus 20:3 (2,5)
4. Matthew 21:42 (5)
5. Hebrews 4:12 (5)
9. Ephesians 5:15 (7)
10. 1 Corinthians 10:13 (7)
12. Romans 12:21 (4)
14. Exodus 3:14 (1,2)

A completed example from "TRYSOR CUDD" (Welsh)

ESIAMPL (13 gair)

L	L	W	Y	B	R	N
F	L	Y	S	D	L	G
I	N	U	E	L	O	Y
W	D	O	S	H	M	T
A	R	M	S	E	A	C
T	N	I	I	A	R	C
I	Y	C	A	M	B	N

→ → (3)....LLWYBR........Y........AC..........

← ← (1)....OLEUNI..........

↓ ↓ ....

↑ ↑ (3)....MAE.......YN.......IM..........

↘ ↘ (2)....LLUSERN.......IM..........

↖ ↖ (2)....DY......AIR..........

↗ ↗ (1)....TROED..........

↙ ↙ (1)....YN..........

Y MAE DY AIR YN LLUSERN

IM TROED AC YN OLEUNI IM

LLWYBR

A half-completed specimen puzzle from "PICSEARCH"

CARROTS

CABBAGE

POTATOES

VEGETABLES (8)

R	P	S	M	U	S	H	R	O	O	M
P	E	C	U	T	J	E	L	L	Z	L
O	A	W	M	C	A	B	B	A	G	E
T	S	J	O	O	N	I	O	N	S	R
A	L	D	Z	L	V	X	E	B	E	E
T	V	Y	E	Q	F	V	V	B	D	G
O	O	J	V	V	W	I	M	Y	C	Z
E	R	Y	S	R	X	U	L	V	B	B
S	R	G	U	D	C	E	U	U	E	V
O	D	U	M	U	F	R	L	D	A	B
S	Z	Y	C	A	R	R	O	T	S	C

PEAS